BEC ━━━

APPALASIAN

BY

LISA KWONG

GLASS LYRE PRESS

Design & Layout: Steven Asmussen
Cover Art: Sarah Rudzunski
Author Photo: Kim Gantt

Glass Lyre Press, LLC
P.O. Box 2693
Glenview, IL 60025
www.GlassLyrePress.com

BECOMING

APPALASIAN

Lisa Kwong's *Becoming AppalAsian* is a generous buffet of delicious family and coming of age poems anchored sublimely by her ABC Sequence. I was still hungry for more after the very last word. The Affrilachian Poets are excited to have our sister poet and these poems at the table. She does the word and her people proud!

—Frank X Walker, author of *Turn Me Loose,*
the Unghosting of Medgar Evers

What astounding "red legacies" sing through Lisa Kwong's *Becoming AppalAsian*! This book carries us from Tai Shan to Indiana, treacherous waters to a bowl of wonton soup that brings together multiple generations of a Chinese family. In these lush narrative poems, Kwong bestows upon us her ferocity and unflappable dignity, inherited from stories about many lifetimes of poverty and flight before her. In this time of escalating violence against Asians in the U.S., this book reminds us to hold our heads up high, to remember where we came from, and to keep on until we reach the proverbial shore of our future, "a home / where there will always be enough to eat."

—Muriel Leung, author of *Imagine Us, The Swarm*

Lisa Kwong's *Becoming AppalAsian* is a lyrical, incandescent interrogation of the American Dream. Shifting effortlessly between China and Appalachia, Kwong's poems are filled with wisdom and authenticity, humor and heartbreak, love and magic. Haunting, poignant and gorgeous.

—Jean Kwok, New York Times bestselling author of
Girl in Translation and *Searching for Sylvie Lee*

Becoming *AppalAsian* is a homage to Lisa Kwong's parents, ancestors, ancestral land, homeland, and chosen land. China influences the cadence through which she experiences all spaces, whether that be Radford, Virginia where she worked as a waitress in her parents' restaurant or in Bloomington, Indiana as an artist and academic in a predominantly white University town. Lisa carries the pride of her father's quest to achieve the American Dream as a Chinese immigrant as well as the triumph and turmoil of defying stereotypes in a western landscape. She is AppalAsian: a Southern woman of Asian descent raised in Appalachia who lays claim to soul food, a Southern drawl, chicken feet, and dumplings. Her poetry offers fresh language to express the complexities of her identity.

—Ciara Miller, author of *Silver Bullet* and founder/CEO of
Miller's Learning Center (Chicago)

CONTENTS

On the 42nd Anniversary of My Father's Swim from China, 10/17/2015

Suspended between shores, you watch your friends
tire, disappear beneath bluish-black waters, never
to resurface. When you agreed to swim together,
you promised to keep going, even if some could not go on.
Someone must reach the shore of freedom. This journey
must not be in vain.

You keep swimming, your family's voices echoing
from the home you left, your son and daughter's faces
etched on clouds. Your limbs grow heavier after the first hour.
You keep time by the shifting sky, one arm, one leg moving
after the other, strong strokes slicing cold Tai Pang Bay.
Salt slides from your eyelashes; the sun is a blinking siren.

Spotting a shark fin in the distance, you quiet your strokes,
your eyes still on Hong Kong. Even the fear of being eaten alive
cannot stop you. You want to live to see your babies grow up,
to grow old with your wife. You must succeed, as a man,
as the head of your family. You keep swimming, believe
your blood father is watching, the father you never knew.

You must keep swimming to rewrite history. His early death
will not be yours. You will live, even though your legs
feel like sacks of rice. You believe there is something
stronger than exhaustion. This is why you continue
to kick towards freedom. This is why you won't stop
until your feet touch shallow ground again.

This is love spanning generations of blood,
red legacies that will survive shark bites, the ghosts
of family secrets. You must keep swimming
to reach the shore where you will be reborn,
a tiger emerging.

Poem for My Mother Who Dared Beyond Tai Shan

You dared to elope after your mother shook
her fist at your husband who would journey
his way out of poverty, out of Tai Shan.
When you received his letter of how he swam
in shark-filled Tai Pang Bay for three hours,
you lit incense in gratitude for his safe arrival
in Hong Kong, not daring to imagine

the what-ifs. Remember the morning when
you found his side of the bed empty, a snake
of fear slithering in your heart. You exhaled
as your babies slept a few feet away. You lit
incense then as prayers for him, yourself,
your two-year-old son, your two-month baby girl,
not knowing when you would see him again.

You hold on to hope as your babies grow strong
with the love of Great-Grandma, grandparents,
aunts, uncles, and neighbors. They babysit
while you raise chickens and hogs to sell.
When you bike on countryside paths
to city markets, your son and daughter ride along,
boisterous about what is beyond your village.

Before putting the envelopes in the mail,
you read your son's letters, carefully penned
characters on thin red and blue-lined paper.
Dear Daddy,
We are well. I am good and taking care
of Mama and Little Sister. We miss you.
Every day your daughter asks, *Where's Daddy?*

And you tell her first Hong Kong, then America.
You watch her captivate neighbors and classmates
with her sticky-toothed talk, hear how she shielded
her big brother from bullies when they mocked

his bulbous head, a fearlessness she inherited
from her father. A child born to parents so poor
no villager wanted to hold him as a baby,

your son soon earns respect when others see
how he zooms through advanced math
on the blackboard, chalk dust flying everywhere.
You are so proud and hope your son succeeds
in life, despite you and your husband having
only six years of schooling. As oldest siblings,
you both had to help support your large families.

One day it is time to leave Tai Shan, your parents,
younger brothers and sisters, friends. You don't know
when you will return; this might be the last time
you see your family. Everyone speaks only beautiful
travel wishes and presses red envelopes into your hands.
Even if you want to cry, don't. You are going to America,
the place they call Gold Mountain, where your husband is.

You must survive the plane ride first. Now nine years old,
your son bounces in his seat, while you and your daughter
vomit into little white paper bags, flight turbulence too much
to stomach as you grieve a little for the home you've left.
But you forget the discomfort when you see your husband
for the first time in seven years. Your daughter,
only two months when he left, loosens

from your hand, runs, and shouts, *Daddy,*
you never carried me on your back!
He laughs, hugging your daughter and son close,
will recall later how he worried before leaving Tai Shan,
This might be the last time I see you.
You and your husband vow to never be apart again
for so long, even though your love has endured
across countries and continents. You both vow
to give your children everything, a world
they won't have to escape, a home
where there will always be enough to eat.

THE BABY BEHIND THE CASH REGISTER AT CANTON RESTAURANT

Ring, ring of the cash register wakes you, but you don't know names for sounds yet. All you hear is noise: strangers' voices, doors swinging, rushing feet. Your mother speaks in a garbled language different from when she rocks you to sleep. Your tiny nose scrunches at all the colliding smells; gas wok smoke, garlic chicken, Szechuan beef, and kung po shrimp float by. Moved to a counter where powdered-face women talk to you in squeaky voices, you begin to cry.

Your whole life will be under spotlights and never meet anyone's expectations: be cute, be quiet, never get in trouble, get straight As, know everything, never feel anything. First American-born Daughter, you carry the bridge between China and America. You are not meant to be ordinary. The way you learn to survive, then thrive: take different worlds and fuse them into a kaleidoscope universe no one has ever seen. Refuse to be written out of history. Tell the world to burn all their Chinese takeout boxes—you won't see the inside of even one.

Blind Spot

Once Daddy left the front door unlocked.
Three years old, I wandered outside
down the front stairs, down the narrow
concrete path not yet ragged after years
of weather and feet beating. I wandered
to the driveway where the long dark blue
Lincoln began to back up. I just wanted
to say goodbye.

Mommy saw the open door. She knew.
She ran, ran to find my small
hand reaching out to touch
the back bumper of the Lincoln.
Daddy braked, sudden, when he saw
Mommy standing behind the car,
slowly holding me up, me waving.
Daddy silenced the ignition.

I was the baby daughter then,
the American diamond daughter,
first American born, showing signs
of spunk and diva, shaking hands
of strangers without fear,
dancing and singing like the birds
I loved to watch through windows.

Today I fear cars backing up
and not seeing me. I curse pedestrians
wearing dark clothes at night.
HOW DO YOU EXPECT ANYONE TO SEE YOU?
I shout inside my car, knowing
they can't hear me.

Mommy hugged me so tight; she could have
crushed me. She tells me her heart almost
stopped. Voice shaking, she shudders
when she thinks what if. She tells me
they lit incense, bowed to the ancestors
for sparing my life.

Tai Shan, Canton Came to Radford, Virginia

At home, there was an ancestor altar in the back room:
framed red signs in Chinese and tarnished brass pots filled
with dirt and burnt incense, stick men in half-hearted prayer,
and a small black and white picture

of a young man who looked like my father.
Eight years old, I asked, *Is this my Dad?*
Ngin Ngin stopped her sewing machine. She told me
it was my real Ye Ye, my father's blood father.

Her face sad and static-crackling like a grainy film reel,
she recounted how soldiers raided their house in Tai Shan,
how she clutched my father, only one year old,
how she saved the picture staring at me

by hiding it in the inner pocket of her pants.
This is all we have left of him.
Ngin Ngin gripped me by the shoulders.
Do not tell your Dad and Mom you know.

She lit a new incense stick in front
of his sole surviving image, made me stand
a few feet away, put my palms together,
then told me to bow three times and say,

Ye Ye, I have been a good girl.
Ye Ye, I have been a good girl.
Ye Ye, I have been a good girl.

Into a loop the incense curled,
unlike the limp, head-bent stick men
surrounding the freshly burned halo.
Ye Ye heard you. He is pleased.

Sundays I wore dresses sewn by Ngin Ngin
and went to Calvary Baptist with my American YiaYia.
There I learned: there is only one God; all others are idols.

This ABC (Appalachian-Born Chinese) Girl

She's a middle finger to the fortune cookie, a middle
child born in Radford, heart of the New River Valley.
Never fully Chinese, she devoured sausage biscuits

before Sunday school; never fully American, she chews
chicken feet, a preference she used to not proclaim, feared
being shamed by white folks grossed out, as if bacon, ham,

and steak were holier. For after school snacks, Mom and Dad made
cheese eggrolls, wok-fried grilled cheese sandwiches. She learned
square dancing in 4th grade P.E., Appalachian English in 7th grade.

She mucks up the model minority parade; no calculus, no physics, yes
clarinet, yes poetry, still voted Most Likely to Succeed. Mountaineer
alumna of Boone, she was raised on Ron Rash, George Ella Lyon,

Donald Secreast, Jim Minick, Rita Riddle, Frank X Walker; now
also reads Aimee Nezhukumatathil, Beth Nguyen, Li-Young Lee,
Marilyn Chin, Celeste Ng, Jean Kwok; carries their words around

like favorite Bible verses. She's got three Southern grandmas calling her
sweetie. Y'all is home, not ni hao. She endures Sis mocking her
sometimes Southern accent, side-eyes Confederate flags who can't see
her Appalachian roots.

Portrait of Appalachian Chinese Girls in Their Grandmother's Garden

Navigating Ngin Ngin's maze
of winter melon and zucchini,
my little sister and I simmered
under the late summer sun
where men zoomed by
in pick-up trucks,
hollering, *Chinese girls!*
like they were hurling
butter knives at our heads.

Ngin Ngin's neighbors,
college boys, liked to bake
themselves on their roof.
We hated college boys.
A swarm of them
worked at Dad's restaurant,
always reeking of sock sweat
and bourbon & coke.
They'd loll around while we ate
Chinese sausage rice, pointing
at us, their laughter, a chorus
of snot trumpets.

Inside the metal crisscross fence,
we meandered as two boys eyed us
from their shingled perch.
Standing up, they yanked
down their trunks, butts
facing us, yelled *Nyahhh!*
and out came their tongues.

The gourds I was lugging
dropped from my arms
onto concrete.
Sis, don't look!
Only four, my little sister stared.
She remembers now,
I wondered what was hanging
between their legs.
I remember the butts.

LEARNING HOW TO CURSE IN TAISHANESE

At Ngin Ngin and Ye Ye's house,
strangers would call, offering this
or that. A child, I was told not to speak

to them. So, I'd hand over
the rotary phone to Ye Ye.
EW...GA...

must have startled the voice
on the other end, but me
and my younger siblings giggled

at the booming and bellowing of Ye Ye's syllables
like inflating giant balloons with black googly eyes
and creepy faces meant to hover over parade floats,

not knowing he was saying
the worst Taishanese curse ever,
the equivalent of motherf**ker.

Later at family dinners,
sometimes Daddy used it
when shouting at Ye Ye,

not his blood father but
the father who raised him
from age two.

The distance between them, while vast,
was not as far as the universe between
Daddy and Real Ye Ye.

Now, when I'm about to pop
off, cursing in Taishanese calms
my inherited temper.

Cursing in English
only makes me feel worse,
as if I've bitten off Lego heads.

Bitten by Bitterness

I.
Carrying an amber cup, Ngin Ngin marched towards me, and I started running. It contained ginseng soup, a flavor too advanced for my immature taste buds. My little feet pounded on the living room carpet to the scratchy porch floor. Nowhere to hide. Cornered on the row of worn surplus restaurant chairs, she forced the cup to my lips. *Drink, drink! Ginseng soup is good for you!*

II.
Once, Ngin Ngin gave me a bowl of ginseng congee for an afternoon snack. At least it had rice and shredded chicken, but its half-bitter taste still frightened me as I stared at the round white bowl with a pinkish rim. I took that bowl of doom, snuck into the main bathroom, closed the door, then dumped it all in the trash, watching the evil soup dribble into darkness. I snuck back out, held out the bowl. *I finished it.* Ngin Ngin smiled, her gold and silver teeth shining, until Sister told her the truth. Ngin Ngin never gave me ginseng again.

III.
I don't fear bitterness anymore. Every time I return home, my parents prepare a gigantic bowl of bitter melon soup. The pieces float in clear broth, little green alligator backs surrounded by sliced pork. This soup doesn't bite; it heals. I've read that bitter melon lowers blood sugar. In Tai Shan, my aunts, Mom's younger sisters, served us bitter melon daily—stir fried with spare rib tips or pork belly in black bean sauce.

IV.
I fear the rising levels of sweetness in my body. Bitter melon isn't ubiquitous like royally dressed desserts that crowd grocery counters and tempt from glass cases at bakeries. What is bitter stuns my mouth, chases toxins away. What is sweet might kill me. One day I could wake up a pile of sugar.

Childhood Fade in Litany

Behind the crisscross fence I thought home was a safe place.
The door's lock loosened. I questioned home as a safe place.
Ngin Ngin took insulin shots and I looked away.

Ngin Ngin had a stroke. Home was no longer a safe place.

Main Street emptied of traffic and home was a safe place.
Smashed beer bottles kept littering the driveway.
Desperate men played lottery at Pak-n-Sak.

I watched her bones become landscape.
Ngin Ngin had another stroke. Home was not a safe place.

Girls cried at the strangeness of incense.
Smoke tendrils crawled down our throats.
My sister and I secretly went to the graveyard.

I questioned God. I asked why home was not a safe place.
Lightning squeezed my hand and home became a safe place again.
I cried at Ngin Ngin's tomb and used to think home was a safe place.

My grief grew a noose. I touched the letters on the tomb.

THE ABC (APPALACHIAN-BORN CHINESE) SEQUENCE

1. The ABC Learns Difference

In first grade,
my classmates wave
ribbon sticks
round and round.
Mark and I sing.
This is not the Chinese
Ngin Ngin speaks at home.
Mark's Mom taught me
the song syllable by syllable.
These words roll around
like gumballs
in my mouth, as I spit them
into the microphone.
After we finish singing,
I look around the gym.
No one looks like me,
only Mark.

2. The ABC Fails After Acing Mandarin in College

Even Mom and Dad mock
my attempts to speak Mandarin.
My desire to keep learning falters
like a limp incense stick.
The nuance of tones fails me.

Every time I meet Chinese natives,
they launch into a language
that sails over my head
like fish eyeballs. I say
Sorry, I can't speak Chinese,
and they gesture and laugh.

I must be a freak.
A cheap imitation,
American-born, the outsider,
the crooked bamboo.

A storm of jade statuettes,
their laughter stones me.

3. The ABC Waitress at Her Parents' Restaurant

A storm of fortune cookies
cracking, your laughter strikes
my ears. What am I, deformed bamboo?
Am I a fraud you can peel
like lychee, an American with Chinese skin?
What if I mocked your Engrish
and requests for suck tubes and tissoos?
I could be a bully, slam your plates
of bok choy down or tell my Dad
to spice up your kung po, so your faces explode in red.
No. I tolerate you, firecrackers popping
inside my lips, as you keep mocking me
in vegetable chopping tones.

4. The ABC Goes to China, 2007

My digital camera sets off
the customs alarm,
keeps me from passing
through to Tai Shan.
The security guards open
my bag, shake out and eye
a half dozen books
and magazines
like they are bombs

ready to detonate.
They finger and flip
through every one,
eyebrows raised
at the topless,
ocean-soaked man
on PEOPLE magazine,
the paperback cover
with a kidnapped girl.
My diary's among the stash.
Will they make me
read my secrets, boot me
out for having a voice?

5. The ABC in the Time of Swine Flu

In a waiting room
in the New River Valley,
you talked to Mom and me
chatting about the weather.
Mom and I switched
into our Tai Shan dialect,
and in ten seconds,
your smile morphed
into an axe, your face
a rugged side
of the Appalachian Mountains.
Y'all from Mexico?
I couldn't respond,
except for a shaky *No.*

The Ex-Waitress Drops a Few Tales

No, I never did spit in customers' food,
but I always cursed sorority girls
and grouchy church ladies who wanted
hamburgers and French fries during Sunday
lunch rush when everyone else ordered
sweet & sour chicken and pork fried
rice. They'd send food back. I'd
scream silently in my head, a clown
smile glued on my face. The Chinese
wanting whole fish and chicken feet
would arrive, oblivious that a dozen
people had been in front of them
in line. They shoved their way
through, started moving tables,
making an island in the middle
of old ladies with pamphlets on how
to get to heaven, of screaming babies
throwing rice on the floor, of Barbie
and Ken families in their frilly dresses
and pressed suits demanding more water,
straws, napkins, sodas with no ice, where's
my extra gravy, I told you no mushrooms,
how many calories. There was the lady
who asked if I was pregnant when I was fat,
the hordes who asked how I lost weight
as if there was some secret to shrinking.
I'd get middle-aged men grabbing my arm,
apologizing before they'd say,
Wow, you've really lost weight!
like it was a miracle skating on egg drop soup.
Maybe it was a miracle. Often customers
would vanish for months, then come back after
they had shrunk, giving in again to the guilty
pleasure they blamed for their waistlines.
A house of a man would eat two cheeseburger meals,
in addition to a family-sized kung po chicken
with burnt black chili peppers. When he was full,

I could see him sweat. I cringed when the snobbish
seafood-loving couple came in, carrying their newspapers.
They'd order fried calamari, a small tub of shark fin soup,
two black bean tilapia meals, and at least two more
entrees. The woman was tiny, her teeth
caked in a black slime. She ate more than women
double her size. I'd clear the plates, she'd walk
to the restroom, and we all knew
what she would do.

Declaration

I used to believe the rumors of who I was.
The smell of ripened bananas. A clumsy kite.
An elephant running into trees and beehives.

They said I fell into a pit of fists, spikes,
and unstrung violins. But I won't sing
their sorrow. In someone's heart

I have not yet been the queen; instead
I've been a reliable doormat, an ear to funnel
pain, a postcard read twice, then stuffed

away. I now rise from a muddy bench
to find peace in a plush love seat.
I will not return to my small hometown.

I won't become someone
mean enough to hate the world.
I now come blessed

like a sidewalk uncracked,
like an ocean unoiled.
Yesterday I was nothing.

Today I am a song
punctuating the sky
like a mermaid's tail.

I Sing to Myself While Driving to Indianapolis Airport

My choir teacher said I was an alto, meaning
I can't scale cathedral ceilings with a whistle
register like Mariah. Forget notes

only dogs can hear. I was never meant to pop
a lung, belting ballads with Whitney bombast.
I sing in my car with its broken CD player.

When crossing county lines and corn fields,
the radio's no use with its static and blurring
of country, pop, and rap. When I sing along

to the divas, I am glittering on stage,
serenading my unrequited, or I am the star
of my own music video, men chasing after me

in rainy streets but never catching up.
On this trip, I am trying to perfect
"Part of Your World," the mermaid's wish

to be human. I remember the summer
before fourth grade when I heard that song
for the first time. Even then I said,

I sing just like Ariel!
There is always desire to be
someone else, everywhere else.

I want to be part of a world where dress size
doesn't dictate the stares of strangers, where
leisure and slowness are not dirty words.

I want more . . . to be where the people are.
I don't want to be with people who make me
belly flop on rocks, who make me feel

like a porcupine in a tutu. I sing the song
of wanting to transcend history
when I sat zippered lip in class

and couldn't measure up to the calculus
geniuses who shared my black hair
but not my size 16 waist.

By the Way, My Dad's on YouTube

Mom hated when Dad stuck his bare
hand in the deep fryer's bubbling pond
to retrieve egg rolls, or when kung fu-ing
on stage, he'd ask college guys to hit him,
every time laughing, their punches
meaningless to his steel stomach.

Mom and I'd sit in the auditorium--
she nervous, whistling inside
like a ready tea kettle.
Born in the Year of the Tiger,
Dad was tough as tiger teeth,
his fists, tiger claws.

At the end of the exhibition,
six layers of cinder
blocks were set before him.
Two guys stood by his side,
were told to touch the stack
to prove this was no

special effects illusion
when his bare palm
tapped the top block,
split and CRASHED
all that concrete
to the stage floor.

Daddies in the South
talk about polishing
their guns on the porch
when their daughters'
dates come to visit.
I'd like to show men
Dad's YouTube video,
but will they stay?

Once a man tried,
and I broke him, broke
him until his masks
fell away, and I could
see his fractured
heart through the mirror
of his boyish tears.

Where You Can See Everything and Everything Sees You

Mom doesn't like cracks of light between the blinds,
keeping them closed to be sure no one sees us. Dad,
not as paranoid, opens windows even in winter.
He shovels snow in a tank top and swimming shorts.

In Tai Shan, Pua Pua hated how poor my father was.
What will you give my daughter? Mom loved Dad
enough to risk her mother's wrath. She snuck out with him,
they exchanged loving glances while working together,

and she read his love letters delivered by their neighbor
with a stutter. Mom joked that their song was "Secret Lovers"
by Atlantic Starr, until I told her it was about an affair.
She loved my father enough to elope. Always huffing,

Pua Pua cursed Dad out for stealing her daughter, gave him
the stink eye when he simply smiled and said, *Hi, Ma!*
I want to know that kind of courage, to love
without fear. Mom doesn't know

about the men who unraveled my world and nearly
destroyed me. These men made me question every lesson
I learned at home and church. I became an angel
with ripped, fading-to-black wings, mascara of morality

dripping down my face. I try to blot the stains,
and it is always the same: I'm peering over the cliff,
wishing I had walked away. Yet who would I be?
A body cannot be unbroken; a spirit can regenerate

if it can find home. Can it survive the hope
in Mom's voice when she asks if I've made progress
with So-and-so? Will I ever love a man enough
to risk everything again, this time in the light?

Declaration Written on a Leaf

I don't want to wait until my skin is a wrinkled leaf
to have love housed in brick
able to withstand a thousand rains. I hollow
out all your secrets, line them inside ringing
clocks where only I can hear your rusted
shame. I know what it's like to fall

into a poisoned pit. I won't wait until the fall
for romance to bloom like summer leaves
green, bright, with veins rustling
to keep alive and not hit brick
walls. Yesterday, I heard you singing
the saddest love song, rain-soaked and low

like a mouth left hollow
of kisses for years. Notes fell
off your tongue, your heartbreak ringing
in my ear. You became a drifting leaf
about to meet its demise under a brick.
Darling, stop your wailing and trust

my love. I know you've trusted
some wicked ones who left you more hollow
than winter branches, turned your heart into brick.
With me, it's okay if you sometimes fall;
I will kiss the stitches on your heart, never leave
you hanging off a cliff, fingers pulsing, tingling.

How can I stop telephones of the past from ringing?
For you, I'll make sure love isn't a busted
safe of counterfeit bills, carry you like the leaf
cradles a ladybug. Let your spirit no longer hollow
in the presence of love. Let it fall
so fully into mine, not even a thunderbolt of bricks

could shatter us. I carry your love in a brick
case; you always bring
me to higher wisdom where falling
no longer hurts. I no longer fear rusted
doorknobs to closed rooms, their threats now hollow.
Every day with you, I'm alive as a budding leaf.

I see us in a brick summer house. Nothing is rusted;
no alarms ring. My body and spirit are never hollow
with you falling into me like millions of blushing red leaves.

An AppalAsian Finds Home
in Bloomington, Indiana

I call myself an AppalAsian,
an Asian from Appalachia.

I rock leopard print and black stilettos,
write protest e-mails to Victoria's Secret,
wear Brooks and flat foot proof orthotics.

After 5K brunch is a French Tickler,
a ham and cream cheese crepe,
mimosa with cherry. I victory-
dance in the basement stairwell
of Ballantine, break into song
upon hearing the word "lonely."

I travel to Greece and Taiwan
vicariously through the men
I liked. I am from letting go
of the man who left for Florida.

I push up and bird dog,
lemon squeeze and tricep dip
as sweat hisses, every breath
a billowing kite lifting my body
higher and sorer.

I keep a flashlight
in the bathroom, just in case
I have to hunker down
in the bathtub
while a tornado blasts
through the parking lot.

I am from tea parties
and Scrabble, Pink Moscato
and Poeteers, exploding tacos,
chicken and dumplings.

I AppalAsian up this Midwest
college town, eat chicken feet,
mac-n-cheese, celebrate butts
and ancestors. I am from
a fridge covered in babies,
none of them mine,
postcards and handwritten poems
received via snail mail.

I ponder the mirror,
study the woman before me,
see the tear-stained tub of lard,
see the runner's legs,
see the glittering, Cinderella
blue earring heart.

S'mores and Smoke

In the pumpkin patch
air, a fire snaps as
speared marshmallows
glide in and out. Flames
catch these delicious clouds,

smoke-kissing them
until they melt, perfect
between the snug hug
of graham crackers
and milk chocolate.

The man with hazelnut hair
and a sunshine heart
kneels and roasts
the perfect marshmallow.
A toasted blush,

it plummets.

Wearing a boyish frown,
he rubs away phantom tears
with his right knuckle
as the perfect marshmallow sinks
into its dry grass and dirt demise.

Gone quick as a leaf twirl,
its loss lingers like smoke-smell
on our jackets, like daily heartbreaks
we carry on a roasting stick.

Searching for Wonton Soup

Nothing compares to Mom and Dad's wontons, mini globes
of ground pork perfectly wrapped in a thin golden skin. But
I can't live at home forever just to be fed. At every restaurant
in Bloomington, Indiana, I try to find a soup good enough:

broth not too oily, skin tender as the meat inside. I love
dozens of crisp scallions floating like emeralds, slick green
baby bok choy steamed just enough. I've been satisfied,
disappointed. Sometimes I wonder what the hell I just ate.

I hate going out to eat with complainers, even though we all can cook
better than what we pay for. Sometimes we don't want to dice
vegetables, or we tire of flipping and stabbing meat with silver
thermometers. We just want to eat. Once in China, my father saw his mother

staring into a soup kitchen window crowded with customers scooping up
wontons and slurping broth, as steam rose to cloud the ceiling. She clasped
her hands behind her back, her face full of hunger. Seamstress money
wasn't enough to buy bowls full of wontons for herself, her husband,

and six children. Dad tells me I don't know struggle, not like they knew
in Tai Shan or when his feet first touched ground in San Francisco, when English
was a diamond locked in a glass case. I will never fully understand their poverty:
imprints on shoulders and hands from carrying buckets of water from a well,

cooking rice over open fire, living in a one room brick house with dirt floor, sleeping
in heat while mosquitoes siphoned their sweet blood. Now filled with gratitude, I know
there are worse things than bad wonton soup. Because they had little, my father
now prepares enough for an army in training: plates overflowing with beef, yu choy,
chicken, broccoli, and shrimp on every table. We fear hunger, fear necessities running
out, so we buy extra, cook extra, wonder: when will anything ever be enough?

Acknowledgements

Gratitude to the editors and staffs of the following journals and anthologies in which these poems first appeared, sometimes in different versions:

Anthology of Appalachian Writers: "This ABC (Appalachian-Born Chinese) Woman"

Appalachian Heritage: "Portrait of Appalachian Chinese Girls in Their Grandmother's Garden"

Banango Street: "Childhood Fade in Litany"

Best New Poets 2014: "An AppalAsian Finds Home in Bloomington, Indiana"

the minnesota review: "I Sing to Myself While Driving to Indianapolis Airport"

Naugatuck River Review: "Tai Shan, Canton Came to Radford, Virginia" and "The Ex-Waitress Drops A Few Tales"

Pine Mountain Sand & Gravel: "Declaration"

Pluck! The Journal of Affrilachian Arts and Culture: "The ABC (Appalachian-Born Chinese) Sequence"

root and branch: "S'mores and Smoke" and "The Baby Behind the Cash Register at Canton Restaurant"

Still: The Journal: "On the 42nd Anniversary of My Father's Swim from China, 10/17/2015," "Blind Spot," "Poem for My Mother Who Dared Beyond Tai Shan," "Bitten by Bitterness," and "Declaration Written on a Leaf"

"Searching for Wonton Soup" was the 2019 Poetry Broadside Contest Winner for Sundress Publications.

Gratitude to The Frost Place, Indiana University Creative Writing MFA Program, and Sundress Academy for the Arts for fellowships and scholarships.

Thank you to Ami Kaye, Steve Asmussen, and the incredible team at Glass Lyre Press for bringing my chapbook vision to life. It's been a joy to work with you all!

Thank you to Sarah Rudzunski for designing the cover art, Kim Gantt for the author photo, Laura Okulski for assisting with the photoshoot, Valarie McDaniel for the photoshoot hair, and Molly Gleeson for proofreading.

Thank you to my poetry sisters: Amanda Foley, Ciara Miller, Hilda Davis, Virginia Thomas, Michelle Deschenes, Evelyn Reynolds, Muriel Leung, Destiny Birdsong. Your love and support have been amazing.

Gratitude to my IU professors, mentors, classmates, and colleagues. Shout out to the IU MFA Alumni Family. Special thanks to Allison Joseph and the late Jon Tribble for their support.

Thank you to the following mentors and workshop leaders who gave generous feedback on earlier versions of these poems: Adrian Matejka, Alyce Miller, Margaret Ronda, Ross Gay, Richard Cecil, Vievee Francis, Gabrielle Calvocoressi, Sally Ball, Martha Carlson-Bradley, Erin Belieu, Steve Scafidi, Rodney Jones.

Special thanks to my mentor Debra Kang Dean for encouraging me to do a chapbook and for supporting me in my various Bloomington endeavors.

Gratitude to my Bloomington Asian and Asian American communities, especially the Asian American Studies Program, Asian Culture Center, and Asian American Association. Special thanks to Ellen Wu, Jennifer Lee, Karen Inouye, Melanie Castillo-Cullather, and Sarah Stamey.

Thank you to my Ivy Tech colleagues for cheering me on.

Gratitude to my students at IU and Ivy Tech for your fantastic work and for inspiring me with your efforts to make the world better.

Thank you to the writers I've met through the Key West Literary Seminar, the Frost Place, and IU Writers' Conference communities.

To my Appalachian regional community, especially the Affrilachian Poets and Frank X Walker, thank you for affirming my work as an AppalAsian poet. Special thanks to Jacinda Townsend, Shauna Morgan, Crystal Wilkinson, Ronald Davis, Mitchell L.H. Douglas, Chris Green, Pauletta Hansel, Jim Minick, Jeff Mann, Theresa Burriss, Marianne Worthington, Lucien Darjeun Meadows, Shayla Lawson, L. Renee, George Ella Lyon, Shawna Kay Rodenberg, and many others.

Thank you to my New River Valley writing group--Chelsea Adams, Carolyn Mathews, Diana Mazor, Lisa Ress, Jeff Saperstein, Mary Ratliff, the late Rita Riddle. Thank you, Donald Secreast, for your friendship.

Thank you to my Appalachian State University community who was so instrumental in the beginning of my poetry education and career. Special thanks to Lynn Doyle, the late Al Young, the late Gerald Barrax, Kathryn Kirkpatrick, Susan Weinberg, Joseph Bathanti, Bruce Dick, Deanna Shelor, Leon Lewis, and many, many others.

To my wider community of writers, thank you so much for all the inspiration and support. Shout outs to Beth Nguyen, Aimee Nezhukumatathil, Jean Kwok, Linda Yip, Stephanie Han, Crystal Meisaan Chan, Tara Betts, Erin Elizabeth Smith, Lori Desrosiers, Jenna Gersie, Stacey Lynn Brown, Laura-Gray Street, Rose McLarney.

Thank you to Writers Guild at Bloomington for all the reading opportunities, support, and promotion.

Thank you to the Bloomington Poetry Slam community.

Special thanks to Maria Hamilton Abegunde, Breon Tyler, Jed Kuhn, Jordache Ellapen, Joe Stahlman, Fileve Palmer, Derrick Robinson, Emily Bedwell, Amy Makota, Ana-Christina Gaspar de Alba, Alli Hart, Derek DiMatteo, Gabriel Peoples, Anna Cabe, Hiromi Yoshida, Jelani Ince, Virginia Githiri, Monique Dallas, Jessica Petersen-Mutai, and Anya Royce for your unwavering support of my work.

Thank you to Molly Hamer and Anne Mahady for your friendship and support during this chapbook process.

Thank you to First United Church of Bloomington for making space for my poems in worship and for welcoming me into your church family.

To Kyle Hetrick, thank you for being an exceptional friend, food buddy, and teaching colleague.

Special thanks to my Godmothers Nancy Schneeloch-Bingham and Wanda Baber. Thank you for cheering me on all these years.

Special thanks to my teachers in Radford City Schools who first believed in my potential.

Special thanks to the employees and customers of Canton Restaurant for 33 years of memories and support for my family. Thank you to my father's kung fu students for their care.

Special thanks to the Cooks, Doves, Weikels, Lees, and so many families for caring for my family in Radford.

So much love and gratitude for my family, especially my parents Simon and May Kwong who worked so hard to give us a beautiful life.

This collection is dedicated in memory of my grandparents: Ngin Ngin, my two Ye Yes, Goong Goong, and Pua Pua.

Glass Lyre Press

exceptional works to replenish the spirit

Glass Lyre Press is an independent literary publisher interested in technically accomplished, stylistically distinct, and original work. Glass Lyre seeks diverse writers that possess a dynamic aesthetic and an ability to emotionally and intellectually engage a wide audience of readers.

Glass Lyre's vision is to connect the world through language and art. We hope to expand the scope of poetry and short fiction for the general reader through exceptionally well-written books, which evoke emotion, provide insight, and resonate with the human spirit.

Poetry Collections
Poetry Chapbooks
Select Short & Flash Fiction
Anthologies

www.GlassLyrePress.com

CPSIA information can be obtained
at www.ICGtesting.com
Printed in the USA
JSHW021219260522
26382JS00001B/52